MENTORING
Cherry On Top!

KAREN MELONIE GOULD

As a Marketing student from the University of Chester I had the opportunity to work closely with Karen for four weeks on a work placement. Her diligence, support and experience have not only pushed me further as an academic, but more importantly have been inspirational and motivational forces that will resonate within me. What I have learned from her will contribute to a professional career for me in the future- no matter where I go. Peter Nathan

authorHOUSE®

AuthorHouse™ UK Ltd.
500 Avebury Boulevard
Central Milton Keynes, MK9 2BE
www.authorhouse.co.uk
Phone: 08001974150

Published by AuthorHouse 10/8/2012

ISBN: 978-1-4772-3106-7 (sc)
ISBN: 978-1-4772-3107-4 (e)

I wish to dedicate this book to all the professionals and businesses that I have mentored or coached over the last four years... Programs – 250 Professionals and over 150 businesses.

'HAPPINESS IS FOUND THROUGH SUCCESS!' OR 'IS SUCCESS FOUND THROUGH HAPPINESS? It is you that measures this journey and mentoring can support that as a tool.

MENTORING – *Cherry on Top!*

TESTIMONIAL –
Jonathan Wright <u>www.wrightwaydigital.com</u>
Details of the Recommendation: "I had the pleasure of having Karen mentor me under the Rock star mentoring scheme. Karen is a highly professional and well experienced business woman with an impressive background.

Through her mentoring Karen has helped me to move forward with my business. She has helped me maintain focus and has already exceeded my expectations in terms of her knowledge, contacts and willingness to get involved."

Service Category: Business Consultant
Year first hired: 2012
Top Qualities: Personable, Expert, On Time

ENDORSEMENT – Jonathan Pfhal <u>www.rockstargroup.</u> <u>co.uk</u> Chaired by Mr Oliver Rothschild – Rockstar have a phenomenal team of Mentors of which Karen is one of them leading on Generating Leads and Team Management, successful in their own right but able to pass on that success to others through Mentoring.

ENDORSEMENT – John Leach – The Founder of Winning Pitch <u>www.thehighgrowthfoundation.co.uk</u> <u>www.</u> <u>winning-pitch.co.uk</u> The High Growth Foundation is a new and exciting membership organization designed to help you grow your business. Our aim is simple, to help hungry businesses develop ways of thinking and behaving in today's marketplace that will deliver growth, fast. We want to make a huge difference and with the likes of having Karen on board as a Accelerator Growth Coach to make this happen!

ANTHONY ROBBINS – UNLEASH THE POWER WITHIN

It's about not waiting any longer. It's about seizing the power that is already within you and challenging you to lead a life of your own design, rather than one that's been scripted by your environment, society or anyone else.

I have just missed his Tour in London in May 2012 and will most certainly make the next one. Whenever, I go to Networking Meetings and meet people who have become successful and who are happy and who I like immediately and they have done it their way not scripted re Text books – they have rather been on one of Tony's Seminars or certainly follow his Strategy.

CONTENTS

CHAPTER 1 – INTRODUCTION

PROFILE – Karen Melonie Gould – HIGH GROWTH COACH/ROCKSTAR MENTOR/Business Angel
<u>www.workbizacademy.co.uk</u>

During 2011, Karen delivered the Department of Business Innovation and Skills Business Start-Up Programme delivering Training and Mentoring support and has supported over 150 new businesses including other programmes, such as Social  Enterprise Network, NWDA, NAVCA, Bank of America and Northern Lights etc. The Bank of America Programme focussed on the growth/development of businesses rather than Start Ups.

Karen is also the Director of www.workbiz.academy.co.uk which supports Professionals and organisations re pre–starts, Business Start Ups and those companies who which to grow and develop their organisations using Work Shops, Master Classes and Mentoring support. Karen is also an Approved Business Coach for the Coaching Consortium for the High Growth Foundation.

Karen is the Director of a Social Enterprise company based in the North West of England www.ccoworkcic.com which has for the past 4 years delivering the Public Sector contracts for Professionals and Executives and has continued to maintain 80% outcomes of securing employment for our clients. Over 250 people are back into work through these programmes, including the Jobcentre Plus Fast Track to Success Programmes which took place in Chester in 2011.

Karen represents Cheshire & Warrington on three Boards in the area – The Local Enterprise Partnership Business Engagement Forums and the Skills Engagement Forum.

As a Rockstar Mentor I support businesses in the NW to develop and grow. Since being on this Programme, I have contacts now in Sri Lanka, Malta, USA, SA and the Caribbean and expanding my network of Export contacts.

Prior to moving to Cheshire, Karen in the 90s had two businesses in the South East – a Professional Introduction Company, Gold Introductions which was featured in many TV/Radio/Magazine media Productions and even starred in her own Reality TV Documentary on Channel 5 which went onto have a combined turnover of £3.4m together with a Training and Business Development Company – Advanced Training securing contracts within the Public sector and working in partnership with some of the TOP FTSE companies in the City re Training, Mentoring and Recruitment.

Karen has also worked in America for their largest Travel Company, Funjet and Funway Holidays where she was the Operations Manager for Jamaica where she lived in the 80's.

MOTIVATIONAL GUEST SPEAKER

Karen is a Motivational Guest Speaker at various Events from the O2 Event in Liverpool 2010 Welfare to Work to 2012 Business NW Event Manchester and Chester SME Event 2012 etc.

CHAPTER 2 – TESTIMONIALS FROM PAST CLIENTS FOR ROCKSTAR MENTORING/COACHING

BUSINESS START UP/PROFESSIONAL

David Keeley MD – <u>www.fidelis.fse.co.uk</u>

This Mentoring/Training Programme enabled me to show how to develop my own business in the UK starting with research, marketing, retraining and finally to grow/develop my business.

My return to the top of the ladder in the Corporate International world has given me both the confidence and drive to do what I do best negotiating international sales and service contracts over all the world whilst still maintaining a successful business here in the UK.

All my aims and objectives to what I wanted to achieve was supported by Mentoring and Karen has enabled me to be the success I am and has even opened the door to me having a business which I thought I never would do.

David McNeilage – Mentee

I joined the Chester Professional Programme and Business Start Up in Oct 2011 after being on Karen's Conservative Party Work/Enterprise Club in Warrington where Karen and I worked for David Mowat MP. I then realised with their support I could start my business. It quickly became apparent that indeed I had two business models which Karen has supported me to develop Though I am presently working in France, I will return to the UK in the Spring of 201 to launch them both with Karen's mentoring support which is invaluable!

Joanne Lyons MD – www.mainstayprocurement.com

I heard through my Social Media network how the WorkBiz Academy had helped others really get their businesses off the ground. On referral, and despite the distance, I travelled up from London to attend the 2 programmes in Chester in October 2011. I found the business start-up programme with Mentoring support, was so worth it as I have now a very successful national Social Enterprise business, Mainstay Procurement.

Karen takes a personal interest in her programme attendees. She even supported me with great contacts in London as; having had a career there for 20 years still maintains a healthy networking and professional presence in the capital.

The programmes have given me the skills to develop my business and the Mentoring support on a 1to1 basis with Karen and her team of mentors gave me the encouragement to start my business based out of London. I am concentrating on growing my business in a sustainable manner with the invaluable support of WorkBiz Academy.

Jane Mawer MD – www.kit2craft.com

I joined Karen's Workbiz/Business Start Up Programme and Professional Programme in Chester in June 2011, following redundancy from a Local Authority. I am Single Mum having to also keep focussed and support 2 teenage boys. The Professional/Executive Back to Work Programme gave me the confidence to start on the Business Start Up programme and pursue my dream of having my own business whilst looking after a family.

The Programmes/Workshops and the intensive on-going Mentoring from various Mentors of my choice, including Karen was a major factor in my business becoming sustainable. Even, when the Programme ended Karen still continued to Mentor me as she does today and has become a friend.

Brian Daintith – Finance Director – Social Housing

I joined Karen on her WorkBiz Club in Sep 2011 in Warrington and then was invited to join her on her Professional Programme for Executives in Chester in Oct 0211. At that time, I was intending on returning quickly to my profession of Finance Director, and was looking for an appropriate opportunity in a blue chip company. At that time, Karen also had another Programme running Business Start up Workshops and even though I did not have the intention of having my own business thought it as an option to explore as when you are unemployed you need all the options that are offered to you. WorkBiz Academy gave me all those options to explore and I finally started my new job in Jan 2012 as a Director of a large service provider to the social housing sector.

Through Karen's Programmes, I also opted for additional support of Mentoring and Karen and her Team of Mentors supported me on a weekly basis on a 1to1 basis to enable me to put into practice what I had learned on the Work Shops to find employment and start a business. The Programmes and the Mentoring inspired and motivated me to secure my future again and their passion and skills enabled me to secure this great new position that I have and it is local!

Kale Malik – International Guest Speaker, Author – US Base – www.kal-malik.com

I have enjoyed being on and working with Karen's mentoring programme for over two years. Karen's brand of mentoring helped me on all levels.

She and her team have skills in many areas of business and personal development. Whether it is finance, interviews or confidence, Karen has the answers.

It helped me to take my career opportunities to the next level. In return I was able to help Karen and her mentees on a few occasions. Karen and her group of mentors have played a great part in me launching my career in personal and professional development.

Head Hunted for an American Company based in the South of England for a Senior IT Role and now living and working in New York, USA as a Guest Speaker, Author and Facilitator of Work Shops.

Natasha Boojihawan – Director at
www.mediastreetmediaarts.com

'Karen really helped me to put my own work into perspective and develop my thinking around how I could drive it forward. Now I can look back and really see what a difference it has made, my business is expanding, and I've taken on new staff and am planning lots of innovative projects.'
   Pavlinia – European Client – Business Start Up Program and Executive/Professional

I have not sold my house, but can't wait any longer. Have accountancy job working for Tristone Flotech international company but based in Liberec, town close by my parents.

I am sorry that I cannot meet you before I go.

Tari is great, adapted so well in CZ school, I am very proud of her.

Thank you so much for your help, advice and moral support you gave me over last few years. It has been much appreciated.

If you ever want to visit CZ then you have to let me know and we can meet.

CHAPTER 3 – INTRODUCTION TO MENTORING

I have been working as a Mentor on various Programmes for over 20 years, since my days as a Business Mentor for the Prince's Trust in London and only recently stepped down from this role in 2010 due to work commitments. I presently am a Mentor for my WORK/ENTERPRISE CLUB in Warrington which is run by the Conservative Party in Warrington – David Mowat MP for Warrington South and here, I have a TEAM of 20+ Mentors that I have been working with for 4 years now and regularly run Mentoring Training evenings based on ILM Level 5 Leadership and Management – Mentoring and Coaching. I am a Fellow of ILM and deliver Executive/Management Programmes using their standards and units to Level 7. I also run a Professional/Executive Programme, 'FAST TRACK TO SUCCESS' in Chester supporting Professionals back to employment and have an equally brilliant TEAM of Mentors there. Please check out my website: www.ccoworkcic.com / mentors for their details. I also run Business Start up Programmes for the Department of Innovation and Skills in partnership with Warrington Business Venture and the University of Chester – Innovation Centre in

Cheshire and work with the same Team of Mentors to support these programmes.

Certainly, over the last 4 years have come to the conclusion that on any Programme that I write and deliver, that having an experienced, well-qualified and a diverse Team of Mentors adds value to my Programmes and I have measured the statistics to prove that the clients on my programmes move forward at a quicker pace and achieve their objectives of employment, starting their own business or Personal or Professional development in a more defined time span and the outcomes are outstanding as my stats prove – I maintain over a 80% SUCCESS RATE of ALL PROGRAMMES delivered in the last 4 years.

Mentoring as a Tool whether you are the Mentor/Mentee is a way of moving forward with your life and your achievements to give you that personal achievement of PERSONAL EFFECTIVENESS. Mentoring is an 'enabler' to support you to move forward with your life, enhancing the effect you have on your professional and personal life from your work to your home, affecting your relationships and being the TOOL to help you achieve that LIFE BALANCE!

Now in 2012 working as a www.rockstargroup.co.uk/mentors supporting UK SME's re growth and development and as a High Growth Coach with www.highgrowthfoundation.co.uk supporting NW Businesses to grow, I have based this book on my personal experience as a Coach/Mentor for over 20 years' and that of my clients.

CHAPTER 4 – MENTOR/ MENTEE GUIDELINES

Welcome to your Mentor guidelines! These are here to help and support you in your quest to achieve Personal and Professional Effectiveness!

These guidelines are intended to act as a guide for Mentor and Mentee's who are involved in Mentoring Programmes and Workshops. They are aimed at supporting the role of the Mentor by providing useful information and advice and by giving the Mentees an insight into the benefits of having a Mentor.

These guidelines aim to reinforce the information given during the Mentor Programmes through our WorkBiz Academy, however, should you require further information please contact us at karen@workbizacademy.co.uk or visit www. workbizacademy.co.uk.

1. UNDERSTANDING THE TOOLS AND TECHNIQUES USED IN MENTORING

The expected benefits and outcomes for me are all of the above but also for me to develop as a Mentor and to share my 'best practice' with my Mentee. I actually receive personal fulfilment from investing in others and I improve my communication and interpersonal skills continually. I certainly felt most valued as a role model and enjoyed this rewarding challenge. The process formed a two way learning relationship, which I know will continue. I actually went on a learning journey myself and felt that I overcame a learning curve as I went.

I also improved my own process and performance to enhance my work on other programmes. At present I am Mentoring fifteen people so I was able to enhance my thoughts and work with others too. There was certainly an insight into this relationship but I am always cautious of becoming too involved as there were some personal issues and conflicts going on within this organisation. This Mentee did challenge me because she knew 'exactly what she wanted' and she was going to get it!

By writing this I had time out to reflect on our Mentoring relationship and this prompted me to adjust my thoughts and actions at times. It also allowed me to renew my focus on my development and career and in particular the role of Mentoring.

1.1 *Evaluate the use of reflection, self-awareness, dialogue, questioning and listening techniques within Mentoring activities to support behavioural and organisational change.*

Using reflection to evaluate activities that take place within my Mentoring sessions with my Mentee. By using the principles of reflection (BONNERNETWORK) this should be a continuous practice with my Mentee and to date it has been. We have had four face to face sessions and numerous e-learning situations. We will continue this Mentoring pattern until Feb 2011. There has, however, been more e-learning taking place than I would have liked and the Mentee has cancelled three Mentoring sessions due to illness. Reflection should also be connective and a relationship/rapport established. Empathy is important and from the first telephone call I could identify a little of myself with my Mentee as she described her struggles to take her organisation to the next level.

I feel learning has taken place for both us. As the Mentor I noted the changes within the organisation's structure and particularly with staffing issues, I then used reflection techniques with the Mentee to challenge her in expanding on these issues, which were stopping her moving forward. It was uncomfortable as the member of staff who prevented the Mentee from moving forward was a close relative, which makes the professional situation personal. Being reflective is being connective, which forces the Mentee to connect through thought and action and to ultimately acknowledge that this is an on-going process.

Evaluating the use of self-awareness with the Mentee to support her behavioural and organisational change was vital. I feel that that the Mentee was always aware of what had to change and what behaviour was required from her in order for such changes to be implemented. She just needed her Mentor/Enabler to alert her to that and for prompt in making those changes within herself and within her organisation.

Using dialogue to evaluate the impact of Mentoring regarding behavioural and organisational change was for me a challenge to focus on remaining within the boundaries of my Mentoring technique (Sirolli – social and enterprise enabler). The Mentee wanted me to advise her and instructed me to take certain action which she knew she had to take for the survival of her relationships both personal and professional - and for the benefit of the organisation. I therefore used prompting to encourage her to make and acknowledge those decisions and to take the necessary action.

Listening – being reflective, using dialogue to have an impact on behaviour and organisational change. There had to be considerable listening and acknowledging taking place within the sessions to promote effective communication and understanding. Nodding to acknowledge and prompting to continue was necessary as this, I feel, is reassuring to the Mentee. It enables them to be expressive -knowing that you are listening and being non-judgemental. It can be a relief for them to 'air' all and 'share' the burden of what has been stopping the process of change. Thus Mentoring enabled this process to begin.

Questioning – being reflective, using dialogue to continue this impact on the behavioural and organisational change. These questions had to be opened and non-judgemental. They were certainly not aggressive, challenging or loaded statements. I used a technique of repeating the Mentee's statement or question and asking her for the solution and using open ended probing such as...

WHY – WHAT IF – CAN YOU? – PERHAPS – CAN YOU? – MAYBE – SO IF – DID YOU? – CAN YOU?

This then satisfies the Mentee that they have made the decision to take the required action and that they found the solution within themselves. They then have the reassurance of a 'sounding board' to move on and take action to support activities within behaviours and to makes changes within the organisation. In this instance, working with a partner, giving them responsibility that they were abusing prompted the Mentee to take a break away from work with her partner to address these issues. With reference to the organisation there were more meetings such as Appraisals where communication was implemented at a higher level so that both Mentee and the organisation as a whole could move forward.

Cindy Buell – Models of Mentoring in Communication

1.2 The impact of personalities and the impact of the selection of tools and techniques adopted

with the Mentee was for me personally an absolute delight! The matching by SENW was spot on to suit my personality and that of the Mentee. Even though I was hesitant about a request by the Mentee that she preferred to work with a woman from a BME background I engages. I addressed the issue by emailing first to point this out, but as I was keen to work with this young lady I pointed out that I had other qualities and experience which would give her added value. I still stated that I would not be offended if she requested someone else and asked if I could call her to explain further. The third process was the initial introduction which lasted for three hours whereby we established a relationship.

With extensive Mentoring/coaching, counselling and business advice experience, I have a strong personality that can be persuasive. Being aware of this ensures that I do not take over or to give business advice when it is not my place. Fortunately for me the Mentee is of a similar personality and it did not clash. To some extent we were by this in a short period of time – establishing trust instantly. As the Mentee is younger than me and indeed the journey she is embarking on is one that I have been on many times before, I could feel her struggle and her dilemma. I wanted to guide her and support her on this journey of behavioural and organisational change.

Business Partners – Successful coaching and Mentoring – Page 230 – CLASH OF PERSONALITIES. I agree so heartedly with this statement "that matter with how much goodwill existed at the outset – if one is a nit-picker and another a creative ideas person then it will not work." It is voluntary, so relationships should not be forced.

Having established our personalities, I could then decide on the selection of tools to adopt to make this Mentoring relationship a success.

TOOLS

I was on the NWDA Mentoring Programme in February 2010 – Elaine Owen – UK Business Mentor of the Year and the NWDA Business Development Mentoring Programme for Growth 2010 and Bank of America Business Mentor Programme 2010 for Sustainability for Business. There is a PROCESS MODEL there – THE 3 STAGE PROCESS – EXPLORATION – NEW UNDERSTANDING AND ACTION PLANNING and I have incorporated that in this process with this Mentee.

- Read through the Profile of Mentee and note any requests (noted preferred a BME Mentor.)

- Asked myself the question... Can I support and enable this journey?

- Emailed to establish initial contact as soon as the profile was sent – no delays in starting the communication process.

- Rang the Mentee after asking her permission to continue at a suitable time.

- Organised the first INTRODUCTION MEETING for 1 hour. This went on for 3 hours – so I felt rapport was established.

- Followed up immediately with agreed ACTION PLAN (attached for evidence.) I asked the Mentee to sign in agreement and to bring it to the next meeting to follow on from.

- Once Action Points had been covered by both parties I organised a follow up meeting to re-evaluate ACTION POINTS. This was to address those areas not covered and to ASK WHY. Then to move on with progression of the behaviour of the Mentee including changes and organisational change. 2 hour meeting.

- Once Actions have been addressed and valued by both parties we organise a third and final Mentoring Session (2 hours). They are made aware that this is the Summary of the Journey of the MENTORING RELATIONSHIP.

*Please note that in between the above schedule; telephone calls, e-learning, visits to premises and invitations to Events and Presentations to witness the changes within the organisation took place.

TECHNIQUE

I often use Corporate Mentoring – Reversible Mentoring and Blended Mentoring, but in this instance used my preferred method of SIROLLI, which is to facilitate and enable enterprise to take place. It was fortunate for me that on this occasion the Mentee has a similar background to myself and indeed is a Social Enterprise which I am. Using a two pronged approach to develop the Mentee's PERSONAL EFFECTIVENESS to support behavioural change and develop the Mentee's confidence, awareness and communication skills to empower them to drive forward organisational change.

For other techniques please read WORKING WISDOM - 1995 – 5 Basic Principles: Bob Audrey and Paul Cohen.

ACCOMPANYING – SOWING – CATALYSING – HARVESTING

1.3 Identifying when problem solving techniques are used in Mentoring. This enabled me to use my Leadership and Management Skills and to implement my Learning/Training from being a FELLOW of ILM. I noted that my

ability to identify where the problems were was key, though the Mentee was aware of this we were able to jointly problem solve.

Behavioural Implementation – NLP – Technique as used in my Training arena. Neuro Linguistic Programming is thinking and the use of language. It is a strategy for outcomes to implement change and to generate a happy ending!

Organisational Change – Part of a Change Management in Leadership and Management ILM.

QUESTIONS & ANSWERS – Acknowledging the problems, taking on board the facts and appreciating the content. Identify the root of the problem and what caused it in order to take action to find solutions.

ACTION – Creating ideas to take action. Look at what worked and what didn't work. Consider why? Understand the process of the action the Mentee will take. Look at the strengths and weaknesses of the Mentee and the opportunities the action offers. Vitally, flag up any risks.

ASSESSMENT – Understanding the bigger picture including changes of behaviour and organisation. In this instance understanding the balance of power within the structure of the organisation and within oneself i.e. the Mentee's relationships with her employees.

SOLUTIONS – Ensuring that the organisation works in harmony as a whole – The McKinsey 7s Framework.

CONCLUSION – Making sure your change process suits everyone. Consult staff from start to finish to improve processes within your organisation.

David Clutterbuck – Techniques for Coaching and Mentoring

1.4 Explain the different techniques needed when Mentoring individuals.

I have been mainly favouring the SIROLLI method of enabling, though at a closer look I have also used BLENDED MENTORING where applicable. Because we have used a lot of on-line learning and communication due to Mentee having been ill and working from home this has worked well. Tracing Mentoring back to its origins in Ancient Greece, where young men were placed under the supervision of a male relative to enable them to learn core values, Murray (2001) states that this goes back to Medieval Times local craftsman prepared young men to take over businesses.

I have also noticed that during this Mentoring journey I used BUSINESS MENTORING (Formal Mentoring – Furlong Maynard (1995) which has its use in training and learning in the workplace. As I identified that some of the obstacles the Mentee faced were similar to my own experience and having been there I shared my experience to help her overcome those barriers i.e. not being included in local Partnership

Meetings because of the fear of someone new trying to implement innovative new ideas. Indeed Professor David Clutterbuck – Vice President of European Coaching and Mentoring Council and author of twelve books has used this approach with Lloyds TSB – World Bank and many others. I use some of his techniques to deliver my Mentoring Training to a group of twelve Business Mentors who support my WORKBIZ CLUB and Social Enterprise Programmes – using ILM LEVEL 5 Leadership and Management and Coaching and Mentoring.

I also took on board that INFORMAL MENTORING took place – as I have the experience and the skills that my Mentee aspires to and many of these she is working towards. From this process and others I have become self-Mentored which takes considerable discipline and the ability to attend events and network successfully, which I feel I do well. This is quantified by my contacts, networks and contracts.

2. UNDERSTANDING THE NEED TO DEVELOP RELATIONSHIPS TO SUPPORT THE MENTORING PRACTICE

2.1 Analyse what is needed for a successful Mentor relationship.

DEVELOPMENT OF SKILLS FOR THE MENTEE

It is essential to analyse the application form of the Mentee and study history and requests, which I did. I also looked at their own achievements to date and what they wanted out of the Mentoring relationship. I also like to ensure that my Mentoring encompasses a two way relationship and I like to learn and develop my skills as I go. I have achieved this by:

CHALLENGES

When faced with crossing a barrier or challenge i.e. attending a Board Meeting with the Director (her husband) it is important for the Mentee to reclaim her power. I took this scenario to the Mentoring Group - SENW Liverpool to reassure me that the decision to not attend was the right one and to ensure the group were comfortable with this.

ESTABLISH A RAPPORT & EMPATHY UPON CONTACT

It is vital to encourage accountability in my role as Mentor. Upon meeting be flexible to adapt to the change of circumstances throughout the Mentoring process. Change strategies according to the needs of the Mentee. Enable them to think for themselves by drawing them out - sometimes even out of their comfort zone. Encourage at all times to become reliant and independent.

SHARING

Allow them to lay out before you all their experiences and skills. Then by communication - probing and asking questions – empower them to find their own solution!

ROLE MODEL

I would like to think that I had become a Role Model due to overcoming my own struggles. This experience has enabled me to offer examples, which in turn the Mentee can observe and hopefully learn from.

FOCUS ON GOALS

You are the 'sounding board' for the Mentee and you must listen! Ask probing questions with short and long-term objectives and as this is not a race the Mentor is not put under pressure. Mentoring is not about creating a stressful environment with anxiety about the delivery of immediate results. It then allows the Mentee to focus on ultimate goals and ambitions.

SUPPORT

The Mentor has entered into a contract to provide continual support until the Mentee has decided that they no longer require the support. Although there are boundaries to this and the Mentor must know when to let go and walk away.

Louis J Zackary – The Mentees Guide; "My experience is not unique – some Mentors engage in formal and informal relationships - personal and professional – just so they can 'sit at the foot of the master.'

2.2 Identify how to build the commitment of the individual to establish effective mentoring.

From the beginning of the relationship the Mentor and the Mentee must agree how to embark on the Mentoring journey:

EMAIL – Do you want me to phone you?

PHONE CALL – Do you want to meet up for an introductory meeting?

INTRODUCTORY MEETING – Do you want to meet up again to discuss what points have been actioned? Agree Action Points. Establishing goals, challenging assumptions and building confidence in the Mentee and the relationship as a whole.

EMAIL OVER ACTION PLAN – For the Mentee to sign to accept the Contract.

You can sue Sykpe or book Conference calls to demonstrate more of an edge if you and the client are comfortable with this method.

2ND MEETING – Points actioned and points not actioned – Why? Discuss ways of moving forward and schedule Conclusion meeting.

CONCLUSION – The closure of the relationship – ending on a positive high!

Louis J Zackary – The Mentors' Guide and Catherine Young – Educause – "Mentoring is a professional activity, a trusted relationship, a meaningful commitment."

I feel that for the partnership to work you should always strive for mutual benefits and work collaboratively to achieve them. From the start agree on confidentiality and never break this code of ethics. Always be honest but not critical nor judgemental but lead the Mentee to also be honest and come to terms with decisions that they must make, with your support. Continue to listen and learn and never undervalue what the Mentee has to say.

Remember, this is a working partnership where you aim to support goals and achieve those goals.

Actions always speak louder than words and leave on a high with the completion of all actions. Remember to be flexible about achieving goals – because the process is just as important.

2.3 Establish goals and agree action plans with individuals.

Prior to the first meeting my Mentee had already established some goals for herself, though they can be re-visited as sometimes these are unrealistic and are perhaps more of a Business Advisor Role. For example, to want to infiltrate the Third Sector Network within a location and compel them to accept the Mentee's organisation's vision. This was not a role for a Mentor, although we can plan a strategy to enable this to eventually take roots.

MENTEE'S MISSION

Taking on board the above, I did look at the overall development of the goals set by the Mentee – both for the short and long term. To establish those goals, direction had to be delivered and engineered by the Mentor and this should then inspire and motivate the Mentee to achieve what is agreed in the Action Plan. You must try to be open and honest at all times and ask open-ended questions like 'where do you want your organisation to be in five years' time?'

ESTABLISHING GOALS takes planning and preparation. The Mentee needs to show up at the first meeting with an Agenda. Before agreeing an ACTION PLAN take notes including review notes and consider all previous communications before agreeing to the ACTION PLAN with the Mentee.

MENTOR'S MISSION

The Mentor's goal is to agree an ACTION PLAN that over the period of Mentoring the dependency on the Mentor to achieve the Actions lessens as the power is driven by the Mentee.

Before agreeing the ACTION PLAN make sure you pin down the main concerns that the Mentee has about their goals and for both parties to value and understand each others expectations. Build upon the Mentee's confidence through attention to their actions and praise them at the next meeting about completion of Actions. Share 'best practice' information and all your past experiences where relevant to enable the Mentee to achieve their goals as set out in the ACTION PLAN.

2.4 Evaluate individual's engagement with the programme through the mentoring process.

SMART – SPECIFIC – MEASUREABLE – ACHIEVEABLE - REALISTIC – TIMEBOUND

This method would allow me to evaluate engagement through the Mentoring programme.

Meenalochani Kumar talks about focusing for the Mentor to engage successfully.

SPECIFIC – The immediate changes that I noticed were that the Mentee took a break away from her business with her husband to discuss ways of going forward for the benefit of the organisation. As the husband had been made a Senior Director it was causing a conflict of interest in terms of direction and a power struggle. Confusion over leadership, vision, values and objectives was occurring, particularly from the staff's point of view. This lead to a husband and wife discussion about how to manage and deliver Board Meetings. The structure of them was considered by looking at the governance of the organisation and the roles of all staff. Also, with one member of Staff – Peter (Trainer) had been off sick recently due to stress down to the conflicting instructions from the husband and wife Directors. Staff Appraisals were introduced and monitoring of staff absence and clearly defined roles for staff were implemented, including who reports to whom.

MEASUREABLE – All of the above areas are in place and I have been invited to a Board Meeting to observe. I had decided to do this prior to the conclusion of the relationship in January.

ACHIEVABLE – Both parties AGREED that this can actually be done. Although in the beginning the Mentee wanted myself (the Mentor) to play a role in the agreed actions, which I declined, I enabled this to happen and supported the process fully. As facilitator I will observe a Board Meeting prior to conclusion.

REALISTIC – What will change? The changes as mentioned above are in place although I am apprehensive at them remaining because of the power struggle within the relationship of the husband and wife. My concerns are heightened due to the culture of the couple – where women are supposed to be subservient to men.

TIME-BASED – It is in place and I will witness at the January Board Meeting the progress and consider whether it is stable.

Florence Stone – 2004 – The Mentoring Advantage. Did I, through Mentoring, help to create in the next generation a leader and female?

3 BE ABLE TO DEVELOP MENTORING INTERVENTIONS TO MEET ORGANISATIONAL REQUIREMENTS

3.1 Discuss the guidelines and protocols for interventions based on accepted mentoring theory and practice.

The Mentee had already set out a guideline on what she wanted to achieve. It is the Mentee's needs and the Mentee who sets the agenda – it is not for the Mentor to impose any other agenda onto the Mentee which is self-serving – i.e. creating a need for the Mentee to want to continue working with the Mentor by suggesting a role within the organisation for monetary gain. Or for the self-gratification of glory to feed the ego of the Mentor.

To work within the boundaries of the Confidentiality of the Agreement between the two parties. Even though I did take an area to be discussed at the Group Mentor's Training to reinforce that a decision I took was the right one I did not mention names or the company. That was not to be part of the process at the Board Meeting or at the Appraisals but to facilitate them and support the decision that was made by the Mentee.

Working within the guidelines and protocols for interventions based on the accepted Mentoring theory and practice. This was sometimes frustrating for me as I had my day job and the Mentee is an extremely busy Leader of a SME, like myself. She was also ill and took time out to spend with her husband for a holiday, which meant our time together was reduced. Thus balancing meetings and scheduling when we could get together was a little frustrating at times. Also as I had to travel from Hoole to Chester to Manchester to Trafford and tried to tie it in when I had other work in the Manchester area. I was also invited to an Evening Presentation Event, but I had an early start that morning in Wales (breakfast networking) and then was busy all day in Chester so we both had to RESPECT each other's time and responsibilities.

My Mentee had used the services of various programmes like ours and had many Mentors before and I felt she used this to her best ability and that of her organisation to support business development. I encouraged her to take responsibility for this relationship, as her Mentor not Business Advisor although there was synergy and over-lapping. I felt confident, however, that I had empowered her to take full responsibility for the change process within her organisation.

Even though it is necessary to be open and honest there is a 'grey' area where I was not going to be put in a position to give my opinion of a personal relationship and this frequently took root in our Mentoring Meetings. Here I had to put the onus on them by asking probing questions to encourage them to consider things for themselves.

I feel that our Mentoring relationship could have developed more – if time had allowed. What with the run up to Christmas, holidays, sickness and our busy schedules... I would like to continue and I believe that we will, having already networked and invited each other to Events etc.

There was a request from the Mentee that I wish I could have been more supportive of – about cultural change within the area where the Voluntary Sector is concerned. This takes time and although we did start on a strategy to work towards this there is much to be done.

W Brad Johnson and P Charles Ridley 2004 – 'Work around problems that develop the relationship between Mentor and Mentee – what it means to Mentor with integrity and end the relationship when it has run its' course'.

'MENTORING' is off line help from one person to another in making significant transitions in knowledge, work or thinking' - Megginson and Clutterbuck 1995 page 13.

So based on the above theories and practice I felt I had helped another person through an import transition personally and within the organisation. This has enable the Mentee to grow and for them to aspire to be the person they want to be and for the organisation to develop and grow.

3.2 Develop interventions of mentoring to support individual's in the achievement of organisation objectives.

I know I have supported organisational objectives by supporting the Mentee in:

Structured Board Meetings

Staff Appraisals – Stress Management and Monitoring of Absence

Weekly Staff Meetings

Job Descriptions – Duties and Responsibilities

In January 2011 at the Board Meeting I will see whether these will be sustainable.

Where the personal issue lies within the husband and wife relationship I cannot comment though because of their culture I don't see it as a working relationship and my advice as a Business Advisor would be for the husband to leave the organisation for the development and progression of the company. This would provide a better work/life balance and less stress placed upon the staff. In my opinion the Mentee knows that this has to happen but at present it is not going to initiate it.

3.3 Evaluate the effectiveness of the mentoring interventions in achieving organisational objectives.

STRUCTURED BOARD MEETINGS

They are a registered Charity and therefore were given direction to look at Board Meeting structure with the Charity Commission.

STAFF APPRAISALS

I supported monthly appraisals for all staff and I sent them a form which I use to support Training and Development of Staff within an organisation.

STRESS MANAGMENT

Group/Team building social event - I was invited to an evening event, but had other commitments.

MONITORING OF ABSENCE

Linked to STAFF APPRAISALS – an ideal opportunity to discuss with staff why they had been having frequent time off and how it is related to stress in the workplace because of the conflict of leadership.

JOB DESCRIPTIONS

At STAFF APPRAISALS go through the Job Description again and agree with both parties signing a copy of it.

The husband and wife took a break away from work to discuss how to continue working together within the Mentee's organisation for the development and growth of the organisation and for the general well-being of their staff.

I feel this Mentoring process had been effective in all the above areas except the relationship with the husband and wife and this is not a boundary I was willing to cross, although it did have an impact on the organisation achieving it's objectives.

CHAPTER 5 - THE DEFINITION OF A MENTOR

The sharing of their business experience, being supportive, fostering an inspirational relationship based on trust and mutual respect and the shared benefits of both parties. Mentoring is about developing ability and potential in an individual by allowing them to optimise their performance.

Requirements of a Mentor:-

- All Mentors must have completed the Mentor Preparation Training Day.

- Mentors should seek guidance when dealing with a Mentee who has personal issues.

- Mentors are advised not to support more than three Mentee's at any one time.

- A Mentor/Mentee agreement form should be completed at the beginning and submitted to the course trainer at the end of the programme.

The suggested areas of competency for Mentors:

- Establish an effective Mentoring relationship

- Facilitation and commitment to the programme

- Demonstrate respect, trust and integrity

- Assessment and accountability

- Successful Leadership / Management / Business

- Supportive/ Drive / Energy / Motivation / Active listening / Communication

The Mentor's relationship with the Mentee is crucial to facilitate the programme and create an environment to develop the individual Mentee to reach their goals and objectives for attending the programme. An important element of this is the development of a warm and supportive Mentoring relationship through the use of good interpersonal skills. However, forming such a relationship may not always be possible and it is the responsibility of the Mentor to recognise this situation. Alternative ways to maximise the support being offered may therefore need to be explored. An example of this is when the Mentor/Mentee do not gel or another Mentor has the skills to support the goal and objective of the Mentee better.

Checklist for First Mentoring Meeting

Date / Time / Place:	
Length of session:	
What do you need to know?	
Mentee's goals / objectives:	
Frequency of contact:	
Agree boundaries and confidentiality:	
Agenda for next meeting:	

CHAPTER 6 – BENEFITS & COMMITMENT

Benefits to the Mentee being Mentored:

- Increased self-awareness and self-discipline

- Support in transitions

- Provision of a sounding board and feedback

- Increased self-confidence and self-esteem

Mentee commitment:

- Be motivated

- Accept feedback

- Allow open and honest communication

- Have realistic expectations of their own and the Mentors objectives

Contract

Mentor/Mentee agreement to attend and support the programme:

- Sickness absence or being unable to attend workbiz programme. The Mentee should contact the Mentor/ course provider.

- Mentor and Mentee should meet at the earliest opportunity to discuss the support and sign the Mentor/Mentee Agreement Contract (Appendix 1).

Mentor/ Mentee Agreement Contract

Mentee Name:	Mentor Name:
Date from:	Date to:
CCO WORK group/ WorkBiz Academy	Contact details:

Statement of Intent:
At the end of the workbiz programme (*insert name*) will be able to:

- Write a CV and speculative job letters

- Develop interviewing skills

- Communicate effectively and confidently

Mentor Signature: _____

Date: _____

Mentee Signature: ._____

Date: _____

Agreed Method of Contact (phone, email, in person)	Action/Tasks for Mentee:	Date Action Completed:

This completed form will be used to form part of the CCO WORK programs/WorkBiz Programs. Information provided will be treated as confidential and in order to provide statistical data as part of the on-going commitment/assessment of CCO WORK/ Workbiz Academy Programs.

CHAPTER 7 – QUESTIONS & ANSWERS

These are a few of the questions and answers that could arise during a Mentoring session:

1) **Where should I conduct the Mentoring sessions?**

   It is advisable to pick a mutually agreed place such as a Cafe. In order to protect both the Mentor/Mentee you are advised not to conduct Mentoring in the Mentor/Mentee own home.

2) **I have a Mentee who isn't contacting me, what can I do?**

   The Mentee may be busy looking for work OR developing their business or have personal or other commitments. Try to contact by email or phone or discuss during the workbiz session.

3) **I will be on holiday - what should I do to ensure the Mentee is will stay on course?**

   Inform the course trainer and Mentee of the dates you are away. Agree a plan of action for the Mentee to do during your holiday. Ask another Mentor to provide support.

4) My Mentee has personal issues...

As a Mentor you are there to provide support to the Mentee on specific CCO WORK programme sessions. You are not a trained professional with a recognised qualification to give advice on personal issues. Suggest to the Mentee that they seek professional advice or discuss with the course trainer who will direct them to an appropriate support network.

5) My Mentee is not progressing or providing the agreed documents.

Discuss with the individual to find out what the problem is and agree a revised date for completion. In order for the Mentee to successfully complete the CCO WORK programme and receive an accredited ILM certificate the individual must be able to show continued attendance and progression on the programme.

6) Lack of Communication...

Even if you identify the goals, objectives and aims of the Mentoring process there just might not be the empathy established from the start between the Mentor and Mentee. Do not take this personally! You can move on from here by suggesting that another Mentor takes over the role.

CHAPTER 8 - MOVING ON WITH MENTORING AS A TOOL

Mentoring has truly moved on since I first starting using it back in the 90's at Hackney Council working on a Project with Young Black Men and working with Peer Mentors (black men within the Community who could influence through developing a relationship and setting an example.)

It has now moved into the modern corporate world, but the idea remains the same - imparting expertise and knowledge to enable others to develop!

We are here because we want to OPEN DOORS TO PROGRESS – whether you use this in your own career or within your own organisation.

As it relies on empathy in order to build upon a sustained relationship you should let the Mentee choose you and once you have established a rapport MOVE ON to sign a CONTRACT to enter upon a journey together.

The MENTOR becomes your friend and indeed within an organisation like ERNST & YOUNG this tool would enable the Mentee to climb the corporate ladder. A lot of high profile companies like Marks and Spencer's view this as a tool for STAFF DEVELOPMENT.

Between the two of you a STRATEGIC PLAN is commissioned, which should give them insight into other issues and create a clear path for their future.

CHAPTER 9 – MENTOR/MENTEE AGREED CONTRACT

Whether I am Mentoring a Company or an individual I use the following contract to monitor, evaluate and record the elements of the process.

FORMAL CONTRACT

This is an official understanding between the Mentor and Mentee which outlines the main expectations and obligations of the two parties involved.

MENTORING

This measures and records that a mentoring system is in place and tracks the relationship between the Mentor and Mentee to ensure that it is a 'happy' one and that mutual guidelines are being followed.

EVALUATION

This form can be used to summarise the main achievements and setbacks. It also serves to track the aims and objectives of the journey and ensure that they have been met.

Mentor/ Mentee Agreement Contract

Mentee Name:	Mentor Name:
Date from:	Date to:
CCO WORK group/ WorkBiz Academy	Contact details:

Statement of Intent:
At the end of the workbiz programme (*insert name*) will be able to:

- Write a CV and speculative job letters

- Develop interviewing skills

- Communicate effectively and confidently

Mentor Signature: _____

Date: _____

Mentee Signature: ._____

Date: _____

Agreed Method of Contact (phone, email, in person)	Action/Tasks for Mentee:	Date Action Completed:

This completed form will be used to form part of the CCO WORK programs/WorkBiz Programs. Information provided will be treated as confidential and in order to provide statistical data as part of the on-going commitment/assessment of CCO WORK/ Workbiz Academy Programs.

CHAPTER 10 – BENEFITS - CORPORATE MENTORING

There are many benefits for a company which uses Mentoring. Some of the main ways in which Corporate Mentoring can be used are as follows:

PRODUCTIVITY

You can improve your staff's awareness of their roles and unleash their full potential. Improving their performance could lead to greater productivity.

CONTINUITY

As senior members move on from job to job it is then difficult to capture their knowledge to pass down to junior members of staff. If you introduce Mentoring within your organisation then senior members of staff can also pass down their values, work ethics, corporate culture and standards. This process ensures that knowledge transfer takes place.

CHANGE MANAGEMENT

In an ever increasing competitive market this process is inevitable and more frequent than ever. You can guide your staff through it by introducing Mentoring Programmes, particularly through difficult times (double dip recessions- austerity.) This process then prepares your staff for the change, making the path as smooth as possible. This then prepares them to become flexible in this transition period.

INTEGRATE NEW MEMBERS OF STAFF

New members of staff need additional guidance and direction, particularly, in the first 6 months and this process of Mentoring can endorse this. Having a senior member of staff mentor a new member of staff will in the long run save you time and money.

RETAIN QUALIFIED MEMBERS OF STAFF

Any 'FAST TRACK,' ambitious member of staff will obviously move on in his/her career, but if you introduce Mentoring to them, as a tool to support other members of staff then they feel valued and are less likely to move on.

DEVELOPING LEADERSHIP SKILLS

Mentoring can assist in bringing out the best in obvious Leaders and so too in creating NEW

Leaders, by developing their skills through a guided process.

UNDERSTANDING STAFF'S NEEDS

By mentoring less senior members of staff you obtain a greater understanding of the challenges facing those at the lower level and using 'LEAN' techniques of Leadership and Management encourage these members of staff to effect the decisions of the organisation.

LOYALITY

Encourage staff to develop and embrace a Mentoring Program so that they can take control of their staff development and become more proactive within the organisation - from job satisfaction comes LOYALITY!

IDENTIFYING SKILL GAPS

Mentoring also flags up within a Mentee their lack of knowledge or skills in a certain area that the organisation can then address. Without Mentoring this could remain unnoticed and is not a holistic working environment for any organisation.

I also use Mentoring to address the following issues:

- **STAFF DEVELOPMENT**

- **PROBLEM SOLVING**

- **DELEGATION**

- **MANAGING PEOPLE**

- **INTERACTING WITH OTHERS**

A GOOD CORPORATE MENTOR is not egotistical and does it for the benefit of the Mentee and not for his/her own self-worth.

Within the workplace, generally speaking the Mentor is older and further up the corporate ladder than the Mentee. HR Departments that focus on DIVERSITY AND INCLUSIVENESS will match Mentors with younger Mentees.

CORPORATE CIRCLES

Particularly useful to women at work this tool can be used to support new women within an organisation to help them feel more secure in having female role models who can share their strategies with them help them overcome challenges within the workplace.

REVERSABLE MENTORING

This has been used to work with ethnic monitories to find out what it is like to be an ethnic minority within the workplace.

CAREER DEVELOPMENT PLAN

Mentoring can be used as part of an individual's CDP if they agree to it.

FAILURE OF MENTORING

Formal schemes can fail if the Mentor is too close to the Mentee within the organisational structure.

THOSE AT THE TOP

With Management's goal often set on recruitment, Mentors can often prove a useful tool to spot new talent and promote from with.

CHAPTER 11 – MENTORING – CAREER DEVELOPMENT

Within an organization employees sometimes forget about their key achievements as it becomes part of everyday life, though using Mentoring as a tool you can:

- Address biggest achievements within the last 6 months and track these.

- What skills and abilities do you have to demonstrate how you achieved these?

- What is your major achievement in your job so far.

Then… You can work on:

- Identifying tasks for the next 6 months; What needs to be done to reach that objective? What skills the mentee needs to achieve those goals? What expertise the mentee needs to acquire to reach that level? And upon completion of the Mentoring process you can identify where the gaps are.

- Identifying goals to make the Mentee think more carefully about their interests, skills and knowledge. Sometimes the Mentee's long-term goals do not relate to their current position – so ask...?

WHERE DO YOU SEE YOURSELF IN 5 YEARS' TIME?

DO YOU KNOW WHAT YOU HAVE TO ACCOMPLISH TO REACH YOUR GOAL IN 5 YEARS' TIME?

DO YOU USE A 'BENCH MARK' OF SOMEONE YOU KNOW WITHIN THE ORGANISATION OR OUTSIDE WHO HAS ACHEIVED THIS AND HOW DID THEY ACHIEVE THIS GOAL?

EVALUATION/MONITORING

Using the ACTION PLAN you can evaluate the progress and check the objectives have not changed.

CHAPTER 12 – ARE YOU AN EFFECTIVE MENTOR?

This is an exercise to establish whether or not you have been following the process of becoming an effective Mentor, because in my book there is no other type of Mentor than being the above:

Would you please write a paragraph or so about what the following mean to you as a Mentor and how would you demonstrate these qualities: Give an example of when this has taken place?

COMMITMENT

_____

_____

_____

_____

_____

_____

_____

_____

_____

_____

ACTIVELY LISTENING

_____

_____

_____

_____

_____

_____

_____

_____

_____

_____

EMPATHY

_____

_____

_____

_____

_____

_____

_____

_____

_____

_____

SENSE OF HUMOUR

_____

_____

_____

_____

_____

_____

_____

_____

_____

_____

As OSCAR WILDE said; "The only thing to do with good advice is pass it on. It is never any use to oneself."

CHAPTER 13 – COACHING IN ACTION

Over the last four years I have been on so many Mentoring Programs but have not forgotten about Coaching as a technique to inspire, motivate, stimulate and even guide. However, having had my Mentoring hat on this has often transpired as Business Advice – an area I will not go into.

I am not going to get into a deep discussion here over COACHING V MENTORING OR ADVICE etc. Instead I shall leave the Coaching ethics to the experts having met many on my journey. Even though I attended the Coaching Academy Programme and then completed a CMI/ILM Accredited Program, I like to work with what I am comfortable with and what suits the client. I have, for the past four years, preferred MENTORING because it allows me to stay as the 'ENABLER' and put on my business hat. Most of the Programs have been supporting businesses to start up, to become sustainable or to grow and develop!

HIGH GROWTH FOUNDATION COACH – www.highgrowthfoundation.co.uk

The High Growth Foundation is a new and exciting membership organisation designed to help you grow your business. Our aim is simple, to help hungry businesses develop ways of thinking and behaving in today's marketplace that will deliver growth, fast. We want to make a huge difference, both to the future of our members and to the North of England.

The Foundation is a unique blended mix of face-to-face and on-line coaching, networking and advice designed specifically to deliver growth. It is bespoke support which will meet the individual needs of businesses in every sector at every life stage.

Over 1,700 businesses in the North West Region over the past two years have benefited from coaching support delivered by Winning Pitch. The North West High Growth Programme has been widely recognised as having had a profound impact on the performance of companies with a desire to achieve sustainable growth. Tailored support to entrepreneurs, delivered by successful entrepreneurs, has helped companies to achieve breakthrough results and overcome many of the challenges growth companies face. Assistance has spanned the spectrum of strategic planning and operational issues, covering strategy, sales and marketing effectiveness, financial engineering and funding, through to organisational effectiveness and personal development. We are currently rolling out the Foundation across the North of England.

If you are interested in accessing 1-2-1 coaching and consultancy via our panel of Top Class Business Coaches, in the first instance you should contact Heather Lomas on 0161 918 6785 or h.lomas@winning-pitch.co.uk to discuss your needs and to organized an introduction to an appropriate business coach. You can request me personally as your Coach or use another.

I now find myself on the above Government Programme - possibly for the next 6 years – so will have to STEP UP to the coaching method of engaging and delivery.

RECOMMENDATION

I came across this organisation and met this delightful and talented lady, Helen and would like you to follow her website and indeed attend some of her training if you are thinking about becoming a Coach.

COACHING – www.purpletree.org.uk
Helen Reuben - Quote

Many organisations realise that employees demand more than financial gain. They require appreciation, recognition, open communication, clear vision and self-actualisation. Ever-increasing customer expectations creativity, intuition, motivation and integrity are increasingly valued and an integral part of organisational culture. Coaching and aligning the individual's goals with those of the organisation, has become imperative in ensuring excellent performance, a flow of innovation and increased motivation in the constantly changing `world of work.`

Coaching is not advice giving or the coach taking over the discussion by sharing experiences. The coaching role is to enable other people to change and achieve by drawing on their own resources in a professional context. They must motivate, inspire, stimulate and guide.

Coaching is a process where one person facilitates the development and action planning of another person, in order that the person can bring about changes in their work and life.

The coaching cycle is based on a change and development process which involves the following stages:

1. **Establishing the coaching process**

2. **Action Planning**

3. **Implementing the coaching cycle**

4. **Evaluation and review of progress**

Coaching involves the development of key skills for coaching. It requires deep listening. The listener needs to genuinely engage with the people they coach. They need to empathise and challenge.

The coach must be able to recognise the needs of individuals being coached, develop coaching programmes appropriate to meet those needs and to help individuals to achieve their full potential.

We believe that coaching is not a substitute for managerial control. Leaders and managers rarely have the time to control. They have to empower and delegate to create a culture of responsibility and self generated actions. Coaching and Leadership are, in many ways, synonymous. Both work by using relationships and dialogue to generate possibilities, change and growth. Coaching is not a technique. It involves a way of viewing relationships, customers and the world.

In our experience, progressive success-orientated organisations recognise that a culture of coaching is needed to shift the paradigm of management from one of control to a committed, responsible partnership.

PERSONAL RECOMMENDATIONS FOR A POSITIVE COACHING EXPERIENCE

1. Assessing the Coachee

Has the Coachee requested a specific type of Coaching? Or if in a corporate environment did the Manger request a certain style of coaching to fit into the culture of the organisation? Was it to improve skills or performance or both?

2. Establishing Ground Rules

This is a process of the Coaching cycle and the Manager must take the initiative for this process, though the Employee could have approached the Manager for coaching support in one or even many areas then your TO DO LIST has already been set.

3. Putting Coaching Skills into Action

You have to decide to COACH or not to COACH. Maybe the Manager wants this process to happen but the employee is not so keen, maybe will be just wary of the process and feels threatened or on trail, so establish a first meeting as an ICE BREAKER to start and then take the next stage of arranging another Meeting which reflects a Coaching session.

What will you Coach? – though you have not started the process, you can define the areas in which to work on which will benefit from the Coaching. For examples, enrolling on an ILM Management Programme or signing off a Project.

When will you coach? – the frequency of the Coaching sessions must reflect the length of time allocated to the Coaching Programme. On the High Growth Programme it is 7 days over 6 months as an example.

Who will you Coach? Who is directly responsible for the Coaching? Will the Manager supervise or will your Team Leader on the Program supervise? Establish boundaries. Who is responsible for what?

CHAPTER 14 – ROCKSTAR MENTORING SUCCESS STORIES

In February 2012 I was honoured and thrilled to start working as a ROCK STAR MENTOR as part of www.rockstargroup.co.uk. This is the UK's NO. 1 ENTREPRENEURIAL MENTORING GROUP.

As their Mentor I am responsible for the growing and developing of their business to make it FINANCE READY to Fast Track their sales and generate leads thus leading to Profit growth ££!

I would like to share with you 3 businesses that you need to watch!

www.cyberhostpro.com – Chris Danks

Chris is a TRUE Entrepreneur and started his business in his bedroom at the very mature age of 14 and is on his way to becoming a MILLIONAIRE by the time he is 30 and to sell on his business by the time he reaches 35 and retires. It is a Web/Hosting/Server business operating in the NW. He already has a turnover of £3/4 million and wants to supersede this by 2015.

www.wrightwaydigital.com – Jonathan Wrightway

Another TRUE ENTREPRENEUR from the North West who has created many businesses and even leads on exciting International Projects in the Caribbean. Jonathan has now set up a cloud based marketing and media agency in the North East of England and through this Program wants to establish a UK Service with International clients in USA, South America, Sri Lanka, and Malta etc. Once his UK operation is well established he will return to the Caribbean to concentrate on his USA/SA Portfolio.

www.youropportunities.net – Martin Eilbeck

Martin had worked in the Insurance industry for most of his career and having been made redundant decided to launch a company that Makes you a Profit £ - Saves you Money and supports your local Charities by providing access to products and services that are cost effective. Martin is based in the North West of England and wanted to create a concept that will support Communities to grow and to generate income for businesses and save money for the consumer and give something back to the Community.

TESTIMONIAL - Only just started out with Karen, but she's already helped me by laying out a general strategy, and introducing me to some useful networks and contacts. I'm looking forward to long and successful business relationship.

I am giving you 3 examples of our MENTORING JOURNEY for you to follow which enabled the above 3 clients to achieve their potential.

EXAMPLE ONE

Mentoring Report:

Client name:	Chris Danks – Director - Cyperhostpro		
Programme Facilitators:	WorkBiz Academy /Rock Star Group		
Mentor:	Karen Gould		
Session date:	19/3/2012 – 2 hrs		
One-to-one	Email	Phone	Other
Detail other			

Meeting Notes:

ACTIONS

SUBJECT – LIVERPOOL

1. **Awards for Status and Branding – sending you the SEN Newsletter to choose one – I have chosen for you jaen@vanguardcf. com £15k Prize.**

Mentoring Report cont:

2. Groups – now that you have one Blackpool hotel – ask for recommendations and this can be your first group. I am staying in the McHalls Hotel this week and will do some Networking for you.

3. I want you to expand your Networks in Liverpool and am introducing you to Ray/Roy at Pacific Steam and Tony O-Neil at Liverpool Vision(I do not have my meeting with Terry until 16 April – a good day for us to meet after?) There are now a few Network Groups around Creative Liverpool or Liverpool Creative – kin2kin – so check them out to support your own Network group.

4. Revamp your own Network Group in the Café downstairs - expects date to be your first Speaker and support you to network and facilitate.

5. Social Media presence – as discussed taking on David on 1 or 2 days per week for 3 month contracts who I use personally and for Work Shops – I have spoken to him and will introduce you to him. Advanced Social Media Master Class is 13 April 9-1 Chester. Please ask David to build up your Twitter!

Mentoring Report cont:

6. Universities – Liverpool – you need to have a presence there are workshops – Guest Speaker and Events – will send you contacts for you to work on but you have to join these on LinkedIn Groups.

7. Now that you have the link to BUSINESS SCENE from me – you should start to get all the Events. I sent you a London Event today.

Switch is free and the next one is 15 April.

Please also look at www.downtownliverpool.com £280 and Liverpool Chambers £149.

You should always try to negotiate and ask to come along as a Guest first and offer to do a FREE Workshop on your chosen topic.

8. Manchester 17/18 Business Scene - I am Guest Speaker – 17 April – How do we learn at 12.30 pm. We might end up with a Stand?

EVENT

Chester – RIC – 22/23 March – I am at the 23 March 7.30 am.

Wales – SME – Outperform 9-4 pm

Runcorn – Holiday inn 8-12 BSU

Mentoring Report cont:

Crewe – SME – I am Guest Speaker at this

Marketing Chester's next Event is 24 May- come with me as a Guest First.

Chester SME – June 29 Crown Plaza – Guest Speaker

Given you all the Events up to August....

9. And on the note you can take your trip to USA and visit 27 June – Google Event –San Francisco

10. No 10% but a Q/A on your web to capture clients and then offer the 10% - No Free consultations.

11. Please log into www.bbc.co.uk/click new ideas on Market Surveys – as YOUR HEALTH CHECK is outstanding. How to get and keep an audience. Looking at your 'demographic' groups – which I think is 16-24 – 24-32. I normally watch this on Saturday morning at 8 am. On CLICK they also discuss SOCIAL DISCOVERY TRENDS – SXSW – an area for you to explore more. Remember to log into www.prezi.com for Presentations – I will try this as well.

Mentoring Report cont:

> **12. If Rackspace are your No 1 Competitor for Cloud – then you need to follow then and link in with them – remember we will be working on Partnerships.**

Actions from meeting:

Action:	By whom:	By when:
As above to sign off before 16/3/2012	CD	16/4/2012
To discuss further on 16/3/2012		

1. CASH FLOW – I have a meeting with my Accountant on 8 April and have mentioned if viewing my comments on your Cash Flow – to look more closely at reducing your overheads. It is a start that premises and staffing are being looked at by you.

2. LOANS

3. NW England

Date & location of next meeting:

16/4/2012 Regus Liverpool

Mentoring Report cont:

Declaration:

Client signature:	
Mentor signature:	Karen Gould
Date:	20/3/2012

EXAMPLE TWO

Mentoring Report:

Client name:	Jonathan Wright Wrightway Digital Ltd		
Programme Facilitators:	WorkBiz Academy /Rock Star Group		
Mentor:	Karen Gould		
Session date:	18 April 2012 1.3pm 2 hrs - Manchester		
One-to-one	Email	Phone	Other
Detail other			

Meeting Notes:

1. Confirmed company name to stay as same – WrightWay Digital Media – needs to start trading now.

2. Web completed – looking good – very futuristic! No recent Projects – put your Consultancy work there that is applicable.

3. Cic – not necessary – trade as a Ltd Liability Company to start and dismiss Social Enterprise.

Mentoring Report cont:

4. I would like you to look at the PDF of the RockStar BP and with what you produced for me mould this into this for Sep 2012. We will start to work on the BP from the next meeting.

5. Partnership – New Business – Sri Lanka – Partner – RESEARCH FURTHER and give me a BREAKDOWN of the costs of the Project set up ready for the Cash Flow

6. Sending you a file to support Research – noted income only for residents at 28% -does this off-set against your set up costs?

7. Malta – research the Chamber of Commerce book that I gave you and read their Times daily. Please return to me. Contact grants@dconsulta.eu and Mala Chambers who are proactive and have ERDF monies – I do have a contact there. I have contacted both for you and copied you in.

8. Introducing you to Chris as Cyberhostpro to discuss the BUSINESS Proposal I put to you.

Mentoring Report cont:

9. Chris has already looked at the Cayman instead of Trinidad – better prospects re tax etc. But, I have contacted my client who is the FD of Moneymarket.com for an update and will pass on to you.

10. Main Objectives

   Web Design – Digital marketing – International

   Economic impact globally – Trinidad – there are tax relief re GREEN business services/ products

   BRANDING – International – Social Media – Networking – Events

11. Fundraising Strategy – I have cherry picked for your mother to Research and submit bids etc. enclosed.

12. For me to support you and keep you focused – need an update of your Progress monthly.

13. New Business – print Company – want to work on this area next meeting.

14. Marketing Strategy contact www.mba. co.uk Stephen Maher – Express 18/4 Advice on South America re market and contacts – copied you into email.

Mentoring Report cont:

15. STRATEGY – I am conscious that you are not following one and need to secure some TIME MANAGEMENT into your working life. Re those other Projects.

16. New Idea – Training Academy – Newcastle College – research.

17. Next meeting May Thursday May 3 – venue to confirm.

Date & location of next meeting:

3 May 2012 – tbc   TBA

Declaration:

Client signature:	
Mentor signature:	Karen Gould
Date:	19 April 2012

EXAMPLE THREE

Mentoring Report:

Client name:	Martin Eilbeck/Youropportunities		
Programme Facilitators:	WorkBiz Academy /Rock Star Group		
Mentor:	Karen Gould		
Session date:	4.5.2012 10 am Café Com Chester – 2 hrs		
One-to-one	Email	Phone	Other
Detail other			

Meeting Notes:

CHAPTER 15 – MENTORING V COACHING – YOUR PERSONAL CHOICE

Mentors/Coaches that I have the pleasure of working with over the last 6 years that support my many Programs.

Please log onto www.ccoworkcic.com/Mentors or www.workbizacademy.co.uk to see Mentors/ Coaches that support our Programmes.

Below are just a few that have been working with me on my Programmes for the past four years. They have their own business and support others within their own organisations and other organisations to succeed. My MENTORING PROGRAMMES have enabled others to have a career in Mentoring/ Coaching **and to achieve success through LIFE BALANCE.**

Short biography: David Casdagli

Life spent in various guises within the Motor Industry for 45 years, in sales, marketing, customer service etc.

Final job as Divisional Sales Director for Courtaulds Automotive Products. Attracted to job club by the experiences I had when made redundant at the age of 50 - at which point in time I still managed to find a job for the next 15 years!

Short biography: Sheila Murphy

My whole career has been spent working in Personnel and Human Resources in various large and SME industries, including Armed Forces, Unilever and privately owned family Ltd companies. My skill experiences span from recruitment, training and development, coaching, project management, disciplinary and conducting exits of staff.

Chartered Member of the Chartered Institute of Personnel and Development.

Short biography: Paul Walsh

I have worked in training, development and adult education for over 12 years. My current role is based in a university, working as a training officer focussing on developing staff members' professional skills and first line management development. I am also responsible for supporting staff affected by redeployment and redundancy, training and coaching on how to become a better candidate. I have experience of training and development work in the travel industry, the civil service and within contact centres. In addition to training, I have some experience of working in a human resources role and teaching basic skills (literacy and numeracy) to adult learners.

Short biography: Mustapha Koriba

Mustapha is the founder and Director of NasNad International, an international consultancy in Strategy, Operations and Leadership Coaching. Prior to that, Mustapha has held Vice-President and Director Roles with large Global companies (ICI now Akzo Nobel, Rhodia, Crown Cork). Throughout his career, he has had extensive experience working with the major consultancy practices on strategic and operational change programmes across the globe.

He has worked in the Americas, Europe, Asia and Middle East and Africa. Sector experience include: Aerospace, Automotive, Chemicals, Fragrances, Food, Personal Care, Pharmaceuticals/Life Sciences, International Banking, Engineering, Manufacturing, Supply Chain/Logistics and IT.

He has coached and trained over 2000 leaders and managers in Strategy, Operations, Leadership and Change Management and he is an external lecturer with Manchester, Bradford and Hull Business Schools on their executive and MBA programmes.

He is also a Business Mentor with a number of organisations such as the NWDA and the MOWGLI Foundation where the focus is to help people set up and grow businesses. He has helped many people through career transitions and secure a future for themselves – be it employment or starting up businesses.

Mustapha is passionate about making things happen through people.

Mustapha holds a BSc (Hons) in Aeronautical Engineering, PhD (Computer-Aided Design) and an MBA. He is also a Chartered Engineer and a Chartered IT Professional.

Mustapha Koriba
www.nasnad.com
mkoriba@hotmail.com
0776 413 2781

Short biography: Amanda

From humble beginnings, and throughout her long and varied career, Amanda has significant experience in working within both the Public and Private sectors. After starting out in banking, she then moved into Local Government, gaining initial experience within the Finance function and then moving into Social Services – where her interest in social and personal development began. After moving to Scotland, where she stayed for 13 years, and gaining qualifications in Training and Training Management, Amanda helped set up a bespoke training unit for long term unemployed men experiencing literacy and numeracy difficulties.

As the then Training Agency was abolished and taken over by LEC's (TEC's in England) Amanda decided to move into the private sector, working for Keyline – a UK building products provider – as a Trainer, delivering commercially driven training to branch staff in Scotland and the North of England. A planned major change in corporate culture allowed Amanda to immerse herself in working alongside a team of expert consultants to drive the culture change programme forward, and to become a standard bearer of a more open management operating culture that saw profitability increase and staff turnover decrease – no mean feat during the significant economic dip in the construction sector in the 1990's.

When Keyline was acquired by Travis Perkins, Amanda was given the role of UK Training Manager – Sales and Management Skills across the 400 branch network. Achieving a Masters in Business Administration along the way, Amanda ensured that her team of skills and development trainers delivered programmes that maintained ongoing growth and profitability, whilst maintaining the corporate culture that had been so hard won.

A move back down to England also heralded a desire to 'go it alone' and Amanda embarked upon life as an independent Consultant, delivering training packages and, after a period of Mentoring new businesses, delivering direct business support to aspiring entrepreneurs.

Amanda has worked with Trafford Business Venture, Train2000, Enterprise Solutions (now Wirralbiz), Blue Orchid and the School for Social Entrepreneurs –

delivering advice and support to hundreds of clients with a broad range of needs.

She has developed specialisms in working with females, socially excluded groups, Social Enterprises, and creative sector clients, as well as offering Mentoring and personal development support to business owners and their staff.

Short biography: Ken Waters

Ken is now retired having spent the past seven years in establishing and developing two BMW motorcycle dealerships in Scotland.

Prior to working in the motorcycle environment, his entire career was involved in debt collection, an industry which has seen huge growth over the past twenty years. He has held positions latterly as Operations Director and Managing Director with EOS Solutions GmbH, a global player in the debt collection market, and in turn a subsidiary of Germany's largest retailer Otto Versand. He was also a member of the Group Strategic Board.

In a rapidly growing market place, Ken has been involved in establishing new businesses and in the acquisition and mergers of businesses in the UK Ireland and the USA.

He has worked closely with senior personnel within the banking, retail and utility sectors with a focus on credit and fraud prevention. He has also been actively involved in both trade associations, having founded the Civil Courts Users Association and twice President of the Credit Services Association, and forums appropriate to the better communication and understanding of credit and indebtedness.

Ken, during his career and particularly in the establishment of new enterprises, has coached and Mentored management and staff at all levels having the core belief that knowledge and self confidence are key to overcoming all career obstacles. His greatest rewards have been in seeing the people achieving career objectives that which they themselves thought unachievable.

CHAPTER 16 – WORKBIZ ACADEMY – SOCIAL RESPONSIBILITY

In 2007 David Mowat MP of Warrington South asked me to write a Program and deliver within the Community of Warrington a JOB CLUB Program to support local people 'BACK INTO EMPLOYMENT'. David and I had been supported YMCA in Warrington where I worked supporting the most disadvantaged in our Community and indeed I had together with my Associates managed to stage Christmas Ball in Warrington in 2006 at the De Vere Hotel in partnership with Wolves Rugby Club, an Event which I was told by our CEO that this would never be possible! Oh how – I love to prove people wrong! My objective was to raise enough monies to have everyone off the streets over Christmas and in accommodation and have a Christmas that we all deserve. We raised £25k – not bad for something I was told was impossible and no one would support but the Community of Warrington does have a 'BIG HEART'

Out of my professional relationship with our local MP and the Conservative Party, I wrote the Program – 'GET BRITAIN WORKING ' which I turned into a book and was endorsed by Theresa May MP – Home

Secretary and Minister for Women. Out of this initial Program which started out as a Job Club on a Saturday morning which is a Voluntary Club and 5 years down the road – with over 250 people into employment and over 150 people supported into new businesses – as the record goes – 'WE ARE STILL STANDING!'

WORKBIZ ACADEMY

WorkBiz Academy is a non-profit organisation formed to create support for unemployed people and is assisted by Mentors/Guest Speakers who are Professionals within our community.

We aim to make a difference not only in the professional life of people but create a quality of life for them and their families.

We provide Training, Mentoring, inspiration. Motivation and Professional/Personal development for all our members

I am pleased to announce our next Program in Warrington starts on Sep 15 2012 every Saturday from 10.30 -12.30 Work Club and 12.30 – 1.30 pm Enterprise Club at the Conservative Party in Warrington. Come along and meet our Team of Mentors or indeed START your OWN Workbiz Academy in your Community www.ccoworkcic.co.uk or www.workbizacademy. co.uk or email karen@workbizacademy.co.uk for details on how to set this up. We also have a weekly newsletter, Jobs Board – ILM Accredited learning

Program – Guest Speakers from industry and a Grand Presentation of achievement on 7 December at 3.30 pm with Guest Speakers and Awards and not to mention another great Christmas Party. You are welcomed to join us!

AIMS/OBJECTIVES

My aim is by using the model. 'GET BRITAIN WORKING' which I wrote to equip members to have the necessary tools to search for work in this new economic climate and ever changing job market. The Programme is accredited on ILM LEVEL 3 – LEADERSHIP AND MANAGMENT – COACHING AND MENTORING. Through using this Programme, having Workshops to compliment this programme by GUEST SPEAKERS and then to have one to one Mentoring Support from my Team of 12 Mentors which were trained by myself – Introduction to Mentoring – Level 5 – Leadership and Management – Coaching and Mentoring as I am a ILM Fellow and an approved Trainer to Level 7 of these Programmes.

The long term objective of this Programme besides giving them the tools to find and search for work and equip them for interviews and to keeping job – but also to give them the Confidence and Soft Skills re Communication Skills to compliment methods used in JOB SEARCH. I want them to achieve a REAL LIFE BALANCE – building upon their Networking Skills at our Events and participate as a Member of WORKBIZ CLUB in the Weekly Newsletter and the new web to be launched this Friday to act as a Community Forum www.ccoworkcic.com to network and communicate across the UK.

The above Programme has run successfully in Warrington from January 2008 to date and has produced:

7 Programmes – next one starting in 15 Sep 2012

outcome of 84% and a TOTAL of £5.4m contribution towards the economy of Warrington.

CHESTER FAST TRACK TO SUCCESS PROGRAMMES

Due to the phenomenal success of the Warrington Programme I was asked in March 2011 by JCP Chester to run a similar PILOT programme in Chester. I modified the above programmes to run 6 weeks – accredited to an ILM Level 3 Award – Leadership and Management and a Business Start up ILM Level 2 Preparing for Business Enterprise. As in the Warrington Programmes we would offer:

- Pre-employment Training for Professionals/Executives to access employment

- On-going Mentoring/Coaching support which starts prior to starting the programme on a re-selection interview by Karen Gould and the this supports after the programme for a further 6 weeks once they are in their Work Placement or have started their business or need further development on this. (As this Programmes yields high results – there are not many clients left who need a Work Placement).

- Guaranteed Job Interview – All clients have been through a mock interview to prepare for Interviews set up by this Programme and on the Panel are ex HR Director of Unilever and local Directors of organisations to support this. Those left on the Programme will be then set up a Guaranteed Job Interview to follow through.

- For those left on the Programme a WORK PLACEMENT will be offered. We have been working in partnership with the Cheshire Voluntary Association who has now a 'pool' of Professionals to offer SME Public/Third Sector organisations.

- We have are now in negotiations with Employers/Providers of mine for several years who have expressed an interest in offering the WORK PLACEMENTS and GUARANTEED INTERVIEWS.

FURTHER INFORMATION

The units which are accredited through ILM allows the client then to start on their own Personal/ Professional Career Development Plan and they can follow this through either with CCO WORK CIC or local colleges to completed higher qualifications or indeed once they are working through their own companies as this is the most recognised qualification for Professionals and is used by all the top FTSE Companies in the UK.

SUCCESS OF PILOT FOR CHESTER FAST TRACK TO SUCCESS PROGRAMMES

17 Jobs were achieved – 5 new businesses are already trading and 6 are in the process of further development to trade with the support of further Mentoring/Coaching and 5 are on a Work Placement and is being monitored by CCO WORK CIC for another 2 weeks working with our Mentors/ Coaches.

PARTNERSHIP

The government have just chosen www. myworksearch.com as their chosen provider to work with JCP to support Professionals via the internet into employment. We have been working with this organisation since early this year in Warrington and now in Chester and our Chester FAST TRACK TO

SUCCESS Clients provided the data and testimonials for their new on-line programme by giving back feedback to create their GOLD AWARD Package for Professionals. We were giving this FREE courtesy of Richard Alberg, the Director and he has stated that he will continue to give any CCO WORK CLIENTS access to their programmes at a reduced fee. The Gold Award has replaced Mandis and is invalid as a JOB SEARCH TOOL to the HIDDEN JOB MARKET and for those wishing to go self-employed for their Feasibility Study and Research. Though, the GOLD PROGRAMME is going to be sold to Executives for £265 – though if through our Academy, I have negotiated a FEE of £50.

HOW THE WORK ACADEMY WILL ADD VALUE

PRESENTATION AND NETWORKING EVENTS – WEEKLY NEWSLETTER

We also offer the opportunity to attend SOCIAL NETWORKING EVENTS which are coordinated by CCO WORK CIC and to attend their own NETWORKING EVENT re their Presentation of their Certificates – where we invite local companies to have a stand so that our Members can showcase their skills or new business. Our Presentation this July 15 2011 at 12 am at Walker Smith and Way Solicitors was well received and Stephen Mosely MP for Chester presented the Certificates. They have also their very own WEEKLY NEWSLETTER as a FREE MEMBER to the WORKBIZ CLUB

NETWORK that holds a Yearly Event – next one being held 7 December 2012 – Warrington.

I am also working with the Grosvenor Shopping Group to hold JOB FAIRS in Enterprise Week in their Shopping Centres – Chester and Warrington – next one Feb 2013 to support Retail vacancies in partnership with Warrington Business Ventures, JCP Warrington and David Mowat MP for Warrington.

PARTNERSHIPS FOR CHESTER

Our facilitators our Walker Smith and Way Solicitors in Chester where we run the Programmes in a Corporate environment. We also worked in partnership with SCOPE to support adults wanting to access employment. We also have supported Scope have indicated that they would like to continue to work in Partnership re this Programme and we further supported them in July 2011 by raising over £200 putting on a ZUMBA Dance Marathon. We have now been asked to support Charities in Cheshire this summer working in Partnership with Chester Racecourse and through WorkBiz Academy will host a ZUMBA Workshop and monies raised this year will go to Cancer UK.

RECORDED STATISTICS – OUTCOMES – MONITORING AND EVALUATION

All of the above is recorded to an ERDF Level of monitoring and evaluation and all Statistics are sent to be recorded at DWP Caxton House as an on-going part of the Programme.

*GUEST SPEAKERS – example – Paul Mcgee who is a local person and who JCP has used as a Motivational Speaker – John Leach – CEO of Winning Pitch, Gareth Burton – Owner of Burton Beavon Accountants and Scott Fletcher Winner of several Entrepreneur Awards.

This Christmas for 2012 all the proceeds from WorkBiz Club in Warrington will as per last Christmas 2011 go towards YMCA Warrington to support the Homeless over Christmas.

Anthony Robbins – AWAKEN THE GIANT WITHIN – How do you want to be remembered? 'Live each day as is it were one of the most important days of your life.

CHAPTER 17 – EXAMPLE OF MENTORING PROGRAM

The Mentoring Program – the cherry on top!

Leadership & Management Agenda

Drivers

- *Fewer managers in the workforce (13.9% of the workforce compared with 15.3% nationally)*

- *Slower growth in the number of managers (1.1% compared with 3.3% nationally between 2003 and 2005)*

- *Greater skills shortages for management occupations (28.8% compared with 23.4% nationally)*

- *Where management skills gaps are identified, these are relatively significant*

- *Demand Issues and Supply Provision*

Programme Aim

- To support leaders, managers and entrepreneurs to develop their capability and potential to improve their business performance and growth.

- To offer SME businesses a suite of mentoring support that allows them to receive practical long-term support from experienced entrepreneurs and business leaders through effective transfer of knowledge and valued experience.

Workbiz Academy Mentoring Induction for Mentors

So find a partner

Person A thinks of a difficult issue or problem they have not been able to solve in their life to date, it could be work or home related.

Person B supports person A in thinking through and clarifying this issue or problem.

However, one ground rule – Person B is not allowed to TELL Person A the answer, or advise or guide!!

Coaching versus Mentoring

Short - Term

Coach

Skills, knowledge,
behaviours
competencies

Opening
perspectives/
horizons

Mentor

Long - Term

© *Clutterbuck Associates 2004*

Developmental Mentoring

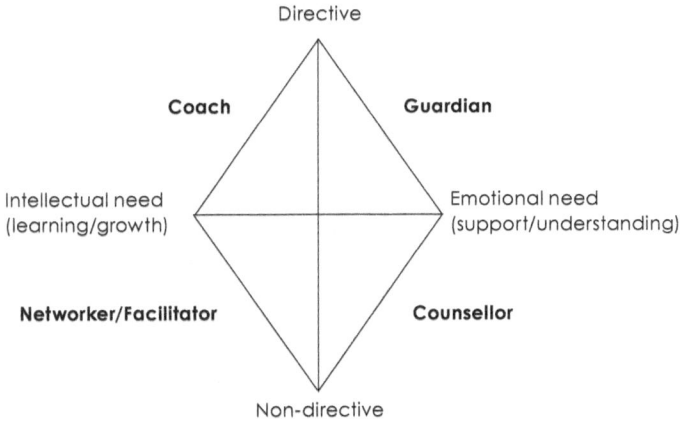

Mentor Helping Roles and Behaviours

COACH (Active)

Goal-setting

Learning

Making casual contacts

NETWORKING FACILITATOR (Passive)

Career Management

Critical friend

Guiding

Challenging

Collaborating

"Bridging"

Catalyst

Sounding board

Role modelling

Career counselling

Listening

GUARDIAN (Active)

Sponsoring

Goals

Mentor Behaviours

Non-Mentor Behaviours

Support

Therapy

COUNSELLOR (Passive)

Self-Reliance

© *Clutterbuck Associates 2004*

So what is Consultancy?

Consultancy is the practice of giving expert advice in a given field. It is intended to clarify a

particular situation or problem with the intention of producing focused advice on possible options.

A consultant can have some influence over an individual or an organisation, but they do not have direct power to make changes or implement programmes.

Our Definition for the Mentoring for Businesses/ Professionals on our Programs:

Mentoring involves an experienced and credible business manager or leader supporting and developing another, through the sharing of their business experiences and the resulting lessons learned.

It is a supportive and inspirational relationship based on trust and mutual respect, and benefits accrue to both participants. Mentoring is about developing ability and potential in an individual allowing them to optimise their business performance.

I am running my next FREE MENTORING PROGRAM based on ILM LEVEL 5 Leadership and Management on July 2012 to support my WorkBiz Academy on 21 September 2012. If you cannot join us in Cheshire join me on-line at karen@ccoworkcic.com and I will send you the program ....NOW – drop down what would make you a Supportive Mentor?

Phases of Reflective Space

External
Energy   Normal Working   Action
             (High Activity)

                               Options

    Framing
        Implication
          Analysis   Re-framing
               Insight!

Internal
Energy   *Time*

Benefits to the individual being mentored

- **Increased self-awareness and self-discipline**

- **Support in transitions**

- **Provided with sounding board and feedback**

- **Accelerated training and development**

- **Expanded personal network and other learning resources**

- **Experience of different options/paths**

- Increased self-confidence and self-esteem

- A safe space to try out ideas

- Access to information

- A source of stretch and challenge

Benefits to the Mentor

- Personal fulfilment from investing in others

- Communication, management and coaching skills

- Enjoyment of a rewarding challenge

- To feel "valued" as a role model

- To stimulate their own learning - a two way learning relationship

- Improve own processes and performance

- Insights into relationship with other people

- Having an opportunity to be challenged

- Opportunity to take time out and reflect

- **Renewed focus on own career and development**

Phases of the Mentoring Relationship

Intensity of learning and value added

BR = Building Rapport

SD = Setting Direction

Progression   Maturation

BR SD   Time

© Clutterbuck Associates 2004

Building Rapport

RAPPORT   **The state of being relaxed with and responsive to another person**

TRUST   **Confidence that the other person is reliable; will respect confidences**

FOCUS   **Concentrating on the individual; listening without evaluating**

EMPATHY   Understanding and respecting the other person's feelings, viewpoints and drives

CONGRUENCE   Building mutuality of objectives; sharing confidence

EMPOWERMENT Supporting, nurturing; absorbing confidence and competencies as steps towards independence

© Clutterbuck Associates 2004

CHAPTER 18 - CONCLUSION

Mentoring and Coaching have become trendy 'BUZZWORDS' and who am I to set the record straight?

In this book, I have tried to set the record straight in terms of my personal experiences of being a Mentor for over 20 years and Coaching for the last 6 years. I have also drawn upon the journeys of my Mentees/ Coaches and other Professionals I have had the pleasure of working with.

It is a process of GIVING and RECEIVING!

I strongly believe that many organisations understand and appreciate the value of Mentoring and Coaching – thus here we are on a Government Programme through the Department of Innovation and Skills (www.highgrowthfoundation.co.uk) for the next 6 years and beyond. Hopefully, as part of this Program we can leave a legacy for future professionals and organisations.

I hope this book as allowed you to focus on your own Personal and Professional achievements as well as those within your own organisation. To remove some of the obstacles which have prevented you from progressing and moving on? From my experience both Mentoring and Coaching yield positive results all round.

I recommend that all Managers, when they embark on their careers, use Mentoring and Coaching to fulfil their life expectations both personally and professionally. I myself had three Professionals Mentoring and Coaching me.

1. **Business Development Mentor**

2. **Life Coach**

3. **Business Mentor**

And, who knows, could in the future engage in the services of a DATING COACH!

Today, in 2012, I only work with no. 1 and still have coffee and an informal chat with both 2 and 3.

As you gain more experience, you will develop the Mentoring skills to pass on to junior staff to ensure that the team members achieve realistic goals. Mentoring and Coaching can also help you as a Senior Executive to evaluate your own skills, identify the gaps and work towards filling them.

Mentoring is one of the most rewarding ways I have found to give back something to businesses and professionals. I reap enormous personal rewards from Mentoring and Coaching as an altruistic act on my part.

If you have shied away from taking on this role in the past then please embrace this process rather as a Mentor/Mentee or Coach/Coachee – as all of these roles are valuable. It is about helping people to reach their FULL potential, contributing to the personal and professional growth of the people and organisations you choose to Mentor or Coach. It is also a personal and professional journey that you take as a Mentor or Coach. This has opened not only my eyes to the way I see the world and people, but my mind to new adventures.

Through my simultaneous personal and professional journeys I have reached maturity in my own development… So come on – what are you waiting for? JOIN ME… karen@workbizacademy.co.uk.

I hope you enjoy this book as much as I did in all the experiences that I had in the last four years of putting this together.

HAPPINESS BRINGS SUCCESS!

Sharing an experience with you… I had a 2 hour Mentoring session with a Rockstar Client yesterday and he was about to go on holiday and to visit his Fiancee and I wanted to give him something that reminded him of our journey together, of how far he had come in terms of setting up his organisation. I bought him a Passport leather case to hold his Passport in – to keep safe and in good condition. As I know how 'love can conquer all' but I wanted to remind him to return to grow and develop his business – as the journey as only just begun!

> **STEPHEN COVEY - The 8th Habit®: From Effectiveness to Greatness**
>
> In today's challenging and complex world, being highly effective is the price of entry to the playing field. To thrive, innovate, excel, and lead in this new reality, we must reach beyond effectiveness toward fulfilment, contribution, and greatness. Research is showing, however, that the majority of people are not thriving. They are neither fulfilled nor excited. Tapping into the higher reaches of human motivation requires a new mind-set, a new skill-set --a new habit. Dr. Covey's new book, *The 8th Habit®: From Effectiveness to Greatness* is a roadmap to help you find daily fulfilment and excitement.
>
> I work with various Mentors/Coaches who use the above method and we are all looking for – above all FULFILLMENT and could we not do with just a little more excitement – yes please – bring it on.

I want to leave you with the quote from Anthony Robbins, 'AWAKEN THE GIANT WITHIN' 'Live fully while you're here. Experience everything. Take care of yourself and your friends. HAVE FUN, BE CRAZY, BE WIRED. Go out and Screw up! .... Page 529

Practice the discipline of CANI!

www.ingramcontent.com/pod-product-compliance
Lightning Source LLC
Chambersburg PA
CBHW051429280526
45785CB00003B/1223